FACING RESOURCE INSECURITY

EAST - CENTRAL INDIANA

SUNNI MATTERS & ROBBY TOMPKINS

THE FACING PROJECT PRESS

THE FACING PROJECT PRESS

An imprint of The Facing Project

Muncie, Indiana 47305

facingproject.com

First published in the United States of America by The Facing Project Press, an imprint of The Facing Project and division of The Facing Project Gives Inc., 2023.

First paperback edition September 2023

Cover design by *Shantanu Suman*

Library of Congress Control Number: 2023943824

ISBN: 979-8-9860961-5-5 (paperback)

ISBN: 979-8-9860961-6-2 (eBook)

Printed in the United States of America

10 9 8 7 6 5 4 3 2 1

Contents

FOREWORD

Bekah Clawson, President & CEO
Second Harvest Food Bank of East Central Indiana

Shedding light on what it is like not to have consistent basic resources for yourself and your family is the main goal of this project. As a Food Bank serving eight counties in East-Central Indiana, we encounter neighbors experiencing food insecurity every day. Often those with food insecurity also experience resource insecurity such as housing, clothing, transportation, money, emotional/mental health support, hygiene and cleaning products, or diapers and baby wipes. Making choices about what is the most important at the moment is not only an unfair choice but also an impossible one.

In the pages that follow, those who are currently experiencing (or have experienced) resource insecurity share their stories. All storytellers have been recruited from our eight-county service area, as have the writers of these stories.

Maybe at this juncture before you jump into reading, we should define "insecurity." It has become a common term in recent years because it is a word that describes where so many neighbors find themselves. It basically means having the feelings of uncertainty and anxiousness about where something might come from, or the results of not having something that is needed.

Some of these stories are very moving and emotional; others are painfully factual. In every instance, however, I am struck that in a perfect world a young boy should not be faced with the prospect of bullying because he has no clean clothes to wear to school; a senior adult should not be wondering where she will live next because she was evicted from her current apartment; and a mother shouldn't have to spend all day at work worrying where she will get food to feed her family for dinner that night.

Another emotion our storytellers have experienced is that of stigma. Not many people I know want to admit to having struggles. If help is needed, being able to access support without being stigmatized for needing it is the optimal desire. Unfortunately, that is often not the case, and in order to receive those resources public scrutiny comes into play and takes a toll on the mental health of the individual or family.

I am not one of the storytellers so eloquently captured on the pages of this book by our amazing writers. I have a story, however, that illustrates having experienced resource insecurity as a child. For all practical purposes on the outside looking in, my family was doing all right. We had food to eat, a home to live in, and clothes to wear. My mom, being a single mom, was able to provide that for her family because we lived with my grandmother who had a nice house that was in a nice part of town with a pension and social security that paid for utilities and food. My mother worked in a clothing store, so with her deep discount clothes were plentiful. What she could not seem to provide was reliable transportation. A decent and dependable car never existed during my childhood. All I can remember were the numerous times that the car overheated—or a tire was flat—or we ran out of gas—or the window wouldn't roll up. The trauma I experienced was fear, embarrassment, and shame that I often still feel in empathy when I see a car stopped on the road or my own car's gas tank is getting toward empty.

Resource insecurity looks so different with each individual. Moving out of resource insecurity is not a linear path. It looks more like the ups and downs of a roller coaster. Resource insecurity is experienced among those in generational poverty as well as those in situational poverty. Indeed, if we really look deep in our lives, everyone has some version of resource insecurity no matter our current or past station in life.

For those reading this book who are providers of resources, and for those who are inspired to try and make a difference for someone, we hope you will take away this message:

Serving neighbors with resource insecurity is not a "one size fits all." We serve different people in different ways, always being sensitive to each individual story and attempting to minimize the trauma and the stigma as much as possible; therefore, closing the resource insecurity gap one person at a time.

EDUCATION SAVED MY LIFE

CORY MATTER'S STORY AS TOLD TO KELSEY TIMMERMAN

I was one of the highest paid prisoners. I got paid twenty-two cents an hour, working on the mop crew at night. I slept in a crowded dorm–seventy beds on one side, and seventy on the other. You could just look out at the horizon of people in cots. It wasn't safe to sleep at night. Anything could happen. There were only two guards who couldn't get there fast enough to protect you. So, while other prisoners slept, I ran the six-person mop crew.

One of the perks was that we got an extra meal and had access to leftovers. I'd give the food to people who needed it.

Food isn't just food. I gave a bologna sandwich and a couple of oranges to a man who was emotionally malnourished. He sat on his bed, in the dark, and didn't say anything. You haven't heard a man cry until you've heard the pain that comes from a man whose wife died while he was in prison.

I felt privileged to be able to put that food where it needed to be.

I slept from six in the morning until two in the afternoon. There were more guards during the day than at night. While everyone was up having to do other things, it would be silent. I would be safe. There would be guards watching.

I was eleven when my parents split up. That was the first time I ever saw food stamps. It was a new thing for me, not just "is there anything in the kitchen that I wanted?" but "where was the next meal coming from?" Food bankruptcy contributed to the emotional bankruptcy that felt its way through stomach pains and made it hard to focus in school. I stole a six-pack of snickers once. I ate one on the elementary school roof. I can't remember the other five, but I hope I shared them. Going days without food has a physiological effect, but the doubt it introduced into my life had an even bigger psychological one.

It wasn't only food; it was also shelter. When we lost our house, I probably lived in ten or eleven different apartments. There were different schools. Different friends.

It wasn't just food insecurity; it was insecurity.

My criminal history with substances started way too early. I was fifteen, going to a school dance, looking forward to breakdancing. You know, I once got a standing ovation from an audience of four-hundred for a breakdance routine I had choreographed. Anyhow, at the school dance, they said I smelled like marijuana. I didn't have any marijuana on me, but they put me on probation for "possession by consumption," which isn't a real thing.

So, I decided to quit school. I filled out the papers and stopped going, but they said the papers didn't go through. They put me in a children's home for truancy. I went through a lot of things, a lot of trauma. I developed substance use issues trying to deal with my feelings.

Things got really out of hand. My life was constantly in jeopardy by my actions and decisions. I went through twelve different rehab programs, which probably is not an exaggeration; some of them court-ordered for up to six months.

Rehab didn't work. I'm not going to talk about the specifics, but I landed in prison, and experienced the diamond pressure of life there. That pressure crushed a lot of people. There were a lot of issues that people were not able to overcome.

My son was born while I was in prison. I realized that if I wanted to meet him, I needed to find a way to live and get out. In prison there's a lot of gang warfare, a lot of power plays. There's the Aryan Brotherhood, there's white supremacists, there's groups based on religious affiliation. There's the Bloods and the Crips. It's all gangs, religion, and race.

I didn't belong to any of them.

I didn't answer the race question on the paperwork when I came into the prison. On my youth baseball team, I had been the only person of color. I was always an outlier, alienated by cultural norms. That's part of who I was. Because of my skin tone, I could've been from any country. People in Muncie thought I was from elsewhere, even though I was born and raised here my entire life. In prison I grew a long beard, and sometimes I would speak with an accent to keep people guessing. I became really pale. So pale that the Aryan Brotherhood approached me about joining them. I told them they would have to kill me where I stood before I joined anybody, because I'd always stood on my own.

But by that point, I had helped so many people from so many of the groups that nobody would allow anybody to mess with me for anything.

I had helped people get their GEDs. And if you got your GED, your time in prison would be cut by six months. I had helped people write letters to their families and lawyers. I had helped people file appeals. I had even developed a curriculum and began teaching a class on philosophy.

Most of the rehab programs I had been through, including AA, focused on character defects. I embraced the idea of developing character assets. I had my own library: Martin Luther King, John F. Kennedy, Mother Teresa, Gandhi. I had been asking myself: *How do I build these character assets? How can I invest in myself?*

I helped others search for these same answers and gave them the philosophical tools and resources to find them.

I had to prove to them, and to the world, that I deserved to exist. I was safe because of the education I had sought out. I was safe because of the education I gave to others.

Education saved my life.

When I sold drugs, I gave people what they wanted and enabled people to destroy themselves. But I came to realize that investing in people is giving them what you know will nurture them.

When I came home from prison there were more issues, and more relapses. But once I realized that I couldn't sacrifice a relationship with another one of my children, I really began to change.

My purpose became bigger than my problems.

I went to Ball State and I just smashed every course. I now have a Master's Degree in social work and am a practicing therapist at Open Door, a federally qualified health center, which means that people with no insurance can be seen. The population that needs the most access is served there. And that's why I wanted to work there.

Food insecurity is connected to so many other types of insecurity, and malnourishment. You can't separate mental health, nutrition, or housing. They all have to be addressed. I think that's a lot of what Second Harvest does with their overlapping programs.

If you have the intellect and savvy to get through a system and thrive, you're almost obligated to try to pass that on. If I could get this education, then there are other people who can, too. Now that I'm in the position to give back, I'm sure never to look down, but to look evenly in the eyes of my fellow humans. Because when we look down on those in need, it shames us all. We need to plant and harvest enough opportunities for everyone.

Ever since we lost our home when I was eleven, I always wore shoes inside the apartments or dorms I lived in. I felt like I always needed to be ready to go, to run. But now that I have a secure home and purpose, I come home, and take off my shoes.

Enjoy your next meal, home, friendship, and the security required to walk barefoot.

I've learned that Cory matters and so do you!

PEOPLE FEED PEOPLE

NEIL KRING'S STORY AS TOLD TO JOSH ZOLMAN

Over Spring Break this last year, a local teacher was talking to some 5th and 7th graders who were at her house. "What would make your life less stressful over the break?" she asked. To help answer the question, she gave the kids some options—having things to do, having transportation to get around, etc. "It would make all the difference," each of them replied without exception, "if we didn't have to hustle for food." We realized that not being in school for these kids meant they would miss out on multiple meals each day. While this is a particular instance where something fell through the cracks, it represents a normal situation that many families in our community face: having access to things they desperately need.

I recently visited some people and communities in Colombia. Amidst a great deal of wonderful experiences, there was one that I continue to think about as I live and walk among my neighbors here in Muncie. I was deeply affected by a cultural difference I have also witnessed in West Africa. They do not have the same sort of system, like we have, for free distribution of food. Everyone, even the very poor, pay at least a little for what they have. However, there is a cultural expectation that if you show up at someone's house, they feed you. This happened over and over, everywhere we went. We would sit down in someone's home, and would not leave without being given no less than coffee, and a kind of fried bread that is common to the area.

Certainly, their culture places a high value on hospitality, but there is a common belief that all people should have food. Instead of systems and structures bearing the weight of setting that up for everyone, they believe that *people* feed people; regardless of how much those people have. In our communities, we are mostly concerned with ourselves; I focus on my own personal opportunities and my advancement. Consequently, there seems to be a cultural adherence to the relationship between what we need, and our ability to work for it—rather than a belief that people's needs are fundamental rights, i.e., food, clothing, shelter; even things we overlook as intrinsically necessary like peace or pleasure. Instead, there is an underlying cultural conviction expressed as, "If you have problems that keep you from having the resources to obtain those things, then maybe you don't deserve them."

Maybe no one would overtly say that, but our structures demonstrate a cruelty that conveys this. So then, there is a subsequent blindness that ignores the many things we all need to be able to acquire resources, in order to live full and whole lives. Unfortunately, in our society, we're alright with that; with people not having enough and it being very difficult to change the trajectory of their life.

We decided to do something different, to begin walking together with neighbors.

We first started doing neighborhood meals at Avondale Church over seven years ago, and our intention was not for them to be about *food*, they were to be about *connection*. It is my own neighborhood, and many people around the community would have described themselves as feeling some sort of isolation, even among neighbors at that time. So, we wanted to bring people together into a friendly environment where connection genuinely happened. When I look back all those years ago at what has transpired from then until now, I can see that most of what we have done has come from the connection made as a result of sharing food together. These times have an even greater significance now than they did back then because we have been able to do so many things as a result of the relationships we have built sharing food together over the years.

These connections have led to life happening, and it happening *together*. Some of this started with faith experiences. When people would come together, we would talk together, and we would sing together. On a December evening, one of our groups stood up and sang *Joy to The World* a cappella. I vividly remember people around the room standing up and joining in. Afterward, person after person, sometimes tearfully, wanted to talk about their experience of growing up in church. The food provided an opportunity for this experience that people have gotten disconnected from. While we can all listen to music on our own, there was something peculiar that happened for people in encountering it together that elicited an emotional response.

Doing communion together is another great example. When people would participate, they weren't receiving it as a traditional church experience. They were receiving communion as a conversation, as a coming together of people who loved each other, and saw each other as equals, and gave of themselves in interesting ways.

Food. That has been the catalyst for all of this.

It is a perfect channel because the truth is people do not have enough. Sometimes they are just looking for food because they need it, but we have found it to be the thing that brings us together. It can be surprising in our community to find people experiencing that kind of hunger, but that is what I find—people that have not eaten in quite a while; days, in fact. So, we help them to understand all of the places right here in our community where they can access food throughout the day and the week; and there is a myriad of ways people can find it.

Unfortunately, there are complications to what a system like this creates. If you live around some of these places that give out free food, you don't actually have to ever buy it. Make no mistake, it takes real motivation and work to orchestrate how to get to all these places. However, there is a kind of dependence that is created. Now, we are in a food crisis, so we are in a good place where, because we have access to resources that our neighbors do not, we can give them what they desperately need. But this is not where we want to end up; this is not the cultural shift I long for where people give to each other because we all believe something I saw demonstrated in Colombia. People want to be able to contribute, to have something they can give to others that have these needs. I see it every day.

I think all of this is related to living in a community with such high rates of poverty. We have many more people who are dependent on acquiring food at little-to-no cost, and need food stamps to make it. We know we are not going to solve complex societal issues with just food. But through the relationships that are being made, we believe we can at least confront the systems at work to keep things this way. What is happening in our city that keeps 30% of the population below the poverty line? We can come together to ask these kinds of questions because in our time together, we've shared space together and learned about one another.

From 5 until about 6:30 on a Thursday night, we continue to see the dawn of good things. We have started a bike shop that kids in the neighborhood work at. We have built a harm-reduction street outreach team. We have empowered people to become community health workers. We started food giveaways during the COVID pandemic. We have given the administrative help people need to fill out forms and complete paperwork to simply get what they need. We've done community advocacy for a crisis center that has given rise to a neighborhood group.

All of this is complicated; it's messy, complex, human. What we are doing may not solve big problems, but we're doing them together. That is how our journey will push further in the right direction. When we start walking with each other, when we pay attention and make sure we all have enough, who knows what will happen?

I want to believe that someday, we will move out of crisis, and into sustainability and thriving. I believe that it may happen when those who are most impacted by the issues become the actual answer to the problem; they will become problem solvers because their dignity has been restored. And that is something worth fighting for.

Gratitude is the Key

Sandra Doyle's Story as Told to Tiffany Erk

I t was cold outside the night that I learned the monetary value of a man's life.

We had just had our seventh child when my husband fell ill. We didn't have insurance so he kept putting off going to the doctor. He just kept getting sicker and sicker until he could barely breathe so we had no choice but to rush to the emergency room. He was weak and struggling to breathe, so I helped him cross the threshold and walk to the admissions area. After an initial assessment, it was determined that my husband required an emergency procedure to survive.

However, we did not have insurance. And that's the moment when everything really changed for us. The hospital refused to treat my husband, my love, my children's father without a hefty deposit of thousands of dollars that we did not have.

My husband gathered himself up and started walking. I asked him what he was doing and he yelled, "I'm going to go out here and lay down and die on these hospital steps, and you sue this hospital for everything they're worth and provide for our family."

This initiated an arrangement with the hospital that allowed for my husband's treatment. He did come home from the hospital, but I will never forget the feeling of being expendable due to poverty.

That night at the hospital was just the beginning of our woes. Our primary breadwinner, my husband, remained ill and unable to work for the next several months. With seven young children at home needing to be fed, I had no choice but to apply for assistance for the first time in my life. The amount of guilt and shame I felt walking into that office is something I will never forget. People judge you and say things like, "You shouldn't have had so many children if you couldn't take care of them." But you never know how your life can change in the blink of an eye.

And so I went, and I pray that nobody ever feels the weight of being unable to feed their children. It is gut-wrenching. I went and I used the programs. Every opportunity for assistance to give us a hand up, I took. And I began to practice gratitude, which is what really turned the tide for us.

Daily gratitude revealed God's awesome presence in my life and things started to change. I noticed that with each passing day, I found more and more to be grateful for! I joined the local Optimist Club to give back to my community and help the area youth. Before you know it, I was elevated to a distinguished leadership position and traveled to a convention in Arlington for the Optimist.

It's been many years since that cold night at the hospital. And as I look back I have nothing but gratitude for all the blessings in my life today. If there is one thing I could say to the world it would be, "Don't lose hope and gratitude!"

IF, THEN . . .

LORETTA PARSONS'S STORY AS TOLD TO SUZANNE CLEM

I f you volunteer long enough . . .

. . . then you might find yourself the director of a soup kitchen one day. Before I'd ever spent a day in the Soup Kitchen of Muncie, which was known as Harvest Soup Kitchen back then, I was part of a group at my church looking for ways to serve others. How could we help our friends and neighbors? Those experiencing homelessness or mental illness, or who were simply in a hard phase of life? We landed on preparing and serving a Sunday meal at the Soup Kitchen. This was around 2006, before I knew anything about food insecurity or food deserts. When a cook at the kitchen left, I stepped in to take on that role. Then when the director resigned in 2011, the Board asked if I'd consider the lead role, and that's what I've been doing ever since. Back when I was volunteering, we'd consider seventy-five guests to be a really busy day. Little did I know I'd see that nearly double over time.

If your community loses five grocery stores . . .

. . . then there will be people who can't get groceries, plain and simple. In July of 2017, Muncie lost five Marsh grocery stores. To put it plainly, I was furious. While two on the north and west ends of town were replaced eventually with Payless groceries, the other three remained vacant, or were bought to become other businesses, like storage. Storage unfortunately does not feed families. The three unreplaced stores were in what I'd consider food deserts. These were also areas where many of our under-resourced community members live, often without cars. People told me what used to be a walk to the grocery store, sometimes daily, was now a stressful bus trip that might take the better part of the day: getting to the bus stop, waiting for the bus, wrangling kids and strollers onto a bus (and then again at a transfer), and then managing multiple grocery bags because you know you can't easily get to the store again any time soon, so you better get as much as you can in that trip. Maybe Dollar General is closer so you now walk there for groceries, and fresh produce stops finding its way onto your table. Maybe you just go without. That July, for several days straight, the Soup Kitchen went from serving about one-hundred-and-twenty-five guests daily to more than two-hundred. I don't know how on earth we did it, but we did.

If we create spaces where people can come into relationship with each other . . .

. . . then we share in each other's losses. Years ago, a regular guest who dealt with alcohol addiction lost his life to it. Other guests asked if we could hold a small memorial service for him. So, we gathered in the dining room. We set up a few pictures of him. We remembered how he would do anything to help someone. I don't think there was a formal service for him anywhere else. We'd come to know him together, and we grieved his loss together.

If we create spaces where people can come into relationships with each other . . .

. . then we also share in each other's wins. One guest used to show up regularly with kids and stroller in tow. Then he landed a job, and eventually he stopped coming to meals. When I'd see him at that job while I was out shopping, he'd give me a big wave. A thrilled wave. You know, sometimes knowing you have a hot meal ready for you in the kitchen frees up time and energy to think about other things, to do other things—like preparing for a job interview. We celebrate those wins together.

If a community rallies together . . .

. . . then we can do big things in hard times. COVID-19 hit just before the Soup Kitchen was slated to hold our annual fundraising event. We had to cancel the event, and as you can imagine, we're wondering how we'll be able to do what we need to do if we can't fundraise. But there were glimmers of hope: we offered our event sponsors the opportunity to receive a refund since we could not hold the event, and all but one sponsor wanted the Soup Kitchen to keep the funds. Even though many people were hit hard financially by COVID, it was a time to reflect on how we could keep each other afloat. With the community's support, we were able to continue serving at the Soup Kitchen by providing cold sack meals to-go, prepared by volunteers who staggered their time in our building to help create safety through distancing. We're so glad to be back to sit-down meals where people can fellowship—where our guests have a chance to take a breath while they share a meal with friends.

If you can dream big things . . .

. . . then you know what you're working toward, even if it feels impossible. My vision for the Soup Kitchen is that one day it wouldn't be needed—that years from now, everyone will have food to eat— every day, without worrying where it will come from. I know that's unrealistic, but whether everyone likes it or not, we are responsible for taking care of our brothers and sisters, our neighbors. The Soup Kitchen is dreaming big by creating a five-year strategic plan that includes broadening services beyond meals. We want to become a space where people can find services to help with all types of needs.

If we pay attention to details that make a difference, like calling the folks we serve "guests" . . .

. . . then we recognize each person's dignity. If we see folks who need a hand up are more similar to others than they are different, then it helps us empathize. If we realize many of our friends, neighbors, and even our own families may be one unexpected expense away from having trouble putting food on the table, it helps us understand that narratives of "lazy" and "not wanting to work" are stereotypes, versus stories. And we're here to be part of people's stories—to help them know their value throughout the whole story, no matter which chapter they're in when they sit down as our guest.

It's A Forever Thing

Brandon Garrett's Story as Told to Melinda Messineo

Forever . . . that's how long my family has been here. Well, actually, if I think about it, my great grandparents moved to Muncie from Wisconsin to work for General Motors (GM). My granddad also worked for GM, and he would have been ninety this year. So, that's a pretty long time. It feels like we have always been here.

I know that people don't understand it, but I love this town, this community. There is a camaraderie here that you don't see everywhere and you can't fake it. When I see my friends from high school, we know we are "shed towners" and no matter where we go, we will always be "shed towners." Even people who moved away are still connected.

It was wild though, when the factories all shut down, so many people left and made it a ghost town here. They were literally here one day, and gone the next. Just pulled up and left their houses and everything in them. Lots of them went to Texas for work and left most of what they had here, like they were going to come back again at some point. Maybe it was more hope than reality that they'd be back, but weeks turned into months, and then into years, and the yards grew up and the houses fell down. Roofs collapsed in slow motion until a house that was fine in Fall, just well, wasn't fine in Spring. Then people started treating the places like they were theirs to squat in and they didn't take care of them, of course. It has been hard to see the neighborhood collapse under the weight of all those neighbors leaving.

That's when the need for food really got serious. The factories left and with them they took the jobs, and with the jobs they took the food, and along with that the family structure that keeps a community going. So many people need food. I just drove by the Ross Center and there were people lined up around the block. There are now four or five churches that give out food. Even my neighbor, Mike, has this open store where you can just come in it and get stuff. He grows the food himself to give to the neighbors, and people come in and get something to eat. You could go in and you can buy a paper heart for a family, and on the back it says what they need and then they deliver it to the family. That's what neighbors do.

There is no shame in needing to eat. I mean, I think all of the schools here have made it so that kids can get free lunch, no questions asked. I remember when I was a kid, if you needed a free lunch, you had to bring this form home and your parents had to prove they needed the help. Who wants to do that? Prove they can't feed their family? Then at the school you had to give them your number and everyone knew you had need and that made it worse, and sometimes the number didn't work so you left hungry and embarrassed. That's awful; that's an ache in your stomach that food can't make go away. I guess it is good now that everyone can get lunch. That seems better, but is it really? I don't know. It seems like things are going downhill.

I remember when the Ross Center was run by the city and the unions. It was great, lots of stuff going on. I remember I was a Ross Center Kid and we went on field trips and had baseball leagues, it was great. We were really proud to have our own team, we were good, and we did good things for the community. We visited the elderly a couple times a month and that was really important. That shaped me into the man I am today. I remember talking to this veteran, an older guy, and he would tell me stories about war and it blew my mind what he did and what he knew. I think it meant a lot to him too, to tell his story, and for someone to be interested in what he had seen and maybe had never put words to before. We would both leave feeling better, like our batteries had been recharged. Kind of like how it feels after you leave church. It energizes you and gives you hope. It's important to share stories across generations like that.

My own work today is like sharing a story across generations. I'm on the city council now and I hold the seat that my grandpa once held. A family legacy I guess you'd say. I knew I wanted to be in politics since I was a little kid. I watched my uncle run for mayor and as soon as I could, I became Precinct Committeeman. Since age eighteen I've held that role. I knew I wanted to be involved because I saw how leaders could help the neighborhood. Like something as simple as fixing a sidewalk or cleaning up a park. This makes people's eyes light up and really improves their lives. I can say that in my role I have helped get safe housing ordinances passed. This gives renters a voice because the landlords now have to keep their units safe and clean. That's all people want; a safe clean place to live, enough food to feed their kids, a nice area to play, and a town to greet neighbors together. We can do that. We need to do that for each other.

As an elected leader, everything I do, I do it for the people. I get asked how we can stop food insecurity and my thought is, we have experts, like the people at Second Harvest, who know what to do. We need to work together, build partnerships, and pull together. We don't need to create new things, we need to support the expert people working hard and help them get things done. We haven't even begun to tap the full potential of what we could do if we worked together. I really respect everyone who wants to lead, but I know that I bring a real passion and commitment that comes from loving this place. This is my home and we are raising our kids here because we love it. I was born here and I will die here and whatever time I have here, I am going to make a difference and make life better for the people, my neighbors. It's a forever thing, you just got to give it your all.

LUMPY MILK

SANDRA CAMPBELL'S STORY AS TOLD TO CARRIE BRADSHAW

There are two things I love most in the world: reading and crafting. Well, I love my family, too, of course, but these are different. These are not only my escape, but also my outlet. I've used reading and crafts to give back to the world in a way that I know how. I didn't have an easy upbringing—between hiding in closets, an empty stomach, and shoes with holes, I had a few obstacles. But with reading and crafting, I was able to use my love of learning to make my life, and others, just a little bit more colorful.

We moved around a lot when I was little. The first home I remember is my grandpa's house. It was my dad's dad's house, and we were staying with him because my dad didn't believe he should have to take care of us kids, that that was a woman's job. (And it's not like we could afford our own house, either.) Grandpa Grove was one of the kindest men I've ever known, and so he stepped up to help look after us. The house had one bedroom and eight people— Grandpa Grove, Mom, Dad, and us five kids. Richard was six, I was four, Bert was three, and the twins were one.

At one point while we lived there, all five of us had the German measles. I don't remember much about that time. I do remember that all five of us slept in Grandpa's bed while we were sick. He helped Mom take care of us. I'm sure we were in isolation from the rest of the world.

When I was five, we moved into the Mayfield Addition house. I have two memories while living in this house. First—the snake. It was my fifth birthday. Dad was mowing the lawn and ran over a garden snake. Richard picked it up and threw it right at me. It landed on my shoulder. I screamed and screamed. I've been afraid of snakes ever since.

My other memory from the Mayfield house was the closet. That's really all I remember of the house itself. Mom would hide us kids in there any time a debt collector came around. There was a steady rotation of them—electric, water, milk. I remember hiding quietly while the Omar man stood outside. Omar sold bread. We couldn't even afford to pay the bread-man. It must have been a big closet if all five of us fit.

When I was six, we moved to the shotgun house. The entire house was three rooms– living room, kitchen, and one bedroom. There was an outhouse in the backyard. Mom and Dad slept on the couch in the living room. Us five kids shared the bunk bed; the two boys got the top bunk and us three girls slept in the bottom bunk.

I remember Christmas while we lived in that house. Two police officers showed up at our door. I was so scared. We didn't know why they were there, but then they revealed a basket full of toys, and we each got to pick one. I picked a set of Christmas cards I could color. I was so proud of being able to give out beautiful cards that year that I had colored myself.

That Christmas, we went to my mom's family to celebrate. There, on the table, was a basket of food for us. The families had all gathered up and got us food. They also bought presents for each of us kids. Dad hated it. His pride was too much. He never joined us for Christmas at my mom's family after that.

When I was seven, we finally bought our first house. It was technically two chicken coops with a makeshift room connecting them, but it was home, and it was ours. With six rooms, it was the biggest house we'd ever lived in. There was a kitchen, living room, bathroom, and three bedrooms (one for Mom and Dad, one for the boys, and one for us girls). We all lived in that house together until they kicked me out at sixteen for getting pregnant.

If you couldn't already tell, we didn't have much of anything growing up. Dad had a ninth-grade education, so when he did have a job, it was at a factory. His paychecks were small to say the least, and what little money he did make went towards gambling and beer. (He always said it was his money.) Whatever was left over after that was used for food and bills. There was never enough left over.

I remember when he'd take all of us kids over to his buddy's house. We'd go over there while he gambled. It was the three men, the three wives, us five kids, Marian's five kids, and Bud's three kids. They'd give us a loaf of bread and a package of bologna to split between the sixteen of us, and that was our meal for the day while the men played cards. And really, the bologna was if we were lucky that day. We could not interrupt them to say that we were still hungry.

That wasn't the only time food was scarce. I remember one time, Dad took us kids to my mom's house for the day. Mom had run off with some man for about a week, so my grandma watched us while he was at work. He woke us up early and fed us an egg. He waited about thirty minutes or so and fed us another egg. Another thirty minutes, and he gave us grits. When we arrived at my grandma's house, he told her that we had already had our three meals for the day, so there was no need to feed us.

Once a month, we'd get commodity food boxes. It was always the best time of the month. We could have a full sandwich each. We'd have fried potatoes, gravy, ham—all in one meal! Even with all that food, though, we did still have to split it. For example, the box often came with six pork chops. Dad would get two pork chops just for himself, and the other four Mom split between her and the five kids. As we got older and were growing bigger, Dad still got his two pork chops.

Even with Dad taking the majority of the food box, it was still the most exciting day of the month every time it arrived. We'd get blocks of cheese, rice, grits, canned ham, and lard. There was often oatmeal in the boxes, but I hated oatmeal. Always have. So, when I'd wake up early to cook breakfast for my siblings, I'd make them oatmeal and me a bowl of grits. The box also always came with powdered milk. Mom never could figure out how to make it. It was always full of lumps. Lumpy milk or not, it was food.

Food wasn't the only scarce item around our house. We often didn't have transportation or proper clothing. Dad was too proud to ever ask for help. If the factory closed or he got laid off, he'd walk to the unemployment office. Even in the dead of winter, he would not ask someone for a ride. So, he'd put on a sweater (we didn't have money for a coat) and walk there. I remember he came back with frostbite on his ears.

Of course, us kids also suffered without proper clothes. There were several times when I had put holes in my shoes. I remember having to cut out cardboard and stick them in my shoes so that I could still walk to school that morning.

That being said, one of my brightest memories is due to clothes. For picture day, Mom made us a pretty skirt. It crisscrossed in the back and came around in the front. I think it had a white background with yellow flowers; I can kind of remember the picture. The skirt was for me and my sister, Bert. I was in the third grade, and Bert would have been in first. I wore it to school first while Bert stayed home. Then, at lunchtime, I ran home and switched clothes with Bert so that she could wear it for her pictures.

I was so proud of that skirt. For one, Mom had made it. She took the time to make us something special, which was not often. The skirt was new and beautiful. It didn't look like all of the raggedy clothes we usually had to wear. This was special.

The skirt wasn't the only thing that made me love school. I just loved learning, and I loved reading. Anyone that knows me now knows that I love to read. I read about a book a day. But I wasn't always like that. You see, growing up, I was not allowed to read for enjoyment. We could read for school, but that was it. I still remember one evening, I was sitting in the living room with a book in my hands. My dad asked me what the hell I had and demanded I throw it out.

Education was not valued in my home. My dad had a ninth-grade education, and my mom had an eighth-grade education. None of my siblings really saw any value in school, but I did. When Bert and I started school together, a week into it, the teachers had me take a few tests. I aced every one of them and was immediately sent on to first grade. (Bert did not pass first grade the first time.) Even when I got pregnant at sixteen and was not allowed to attend normal school, I attended night school and earned my high school diploma.

I think I value education and learning because I wanted to make something of myself. I wanted to be a better person. And I think that shows now. My passion is teaching. I have taught crafts for years and all over the country—well, at least Indiana and Florida. I've taught painting, crochet, knitting, cake decorating, sewing, quilting, plastic canvas, macrame, woodwork . . . You name it, I taught it.

I think it's safe to say that I had a hard childhood. But I did not let that stop me. If anything, it pushed me. It pushed me to be better and to make the world a better place, even if that simply meant teaching someone a simple hand stitch.

Where's Your Cape?

Carol Bradshaw's Story as Told to Carrie Bradshaw

It took me a long time to decide what story I wanted to share. Nothing felt right. But then I realized the exact thing I wanted to talk about—I wanted to share how lucky I've been with my resources. I wanted to be able to thank all of the people who helped me when I needed it most.

The first time that stands out that someone helped me was when I was pregnant. My now-ex (Cain) and I were living in a trailer, and one day in the mail there was a little book of coupons and some money. I remember it saying "Give God the glory." I'm not a religious person, but I was still grateful.

I used the money and coupons to make Cain dinner. I made chicken and noodles, mashed potatoes, and rolls. It was elaborate for the time because it was expensive. I remember my grandmother came over to help me debone the chicken. While I now regret using the money to cook Cain dinner, I am very grateful to whichever stranger left it in my mailbox that day.

For the longest time, we were a family of four living off one income. We had countless medical bills to pay, and we simply did not have the money. Leaving my ex was the best decision I ever made financially (and otherwise), but we still didn't have much. Though we didn't have much, my kids and I got to experience so many fun and exciting things due to the resources I had at hand. My job at the time took us to Indians' baseball games. My friend took us to the VIP box at the Anderson Speedway. My parents took us to the Indianapolis Children's Museum. My kids knew we didn't have a lot of money, but they still got to experience these wonderful things.

Many of my friends at work often gave me money to take the kids to go do things and help provide for them. If there was a field trip coming up, or my son needed new cleats for baseball, or my daughter needed her first bra—they helped.

I remember my daughter was invited to go to New York because she had won a writing competition. We didn't really have the money to go, but she had worked so hard. I wanted her to have that experience. My boss at the time called me into his office. I thought I was in trouble for something, but he said he had heard about our trip. He handed me cash right there to help make it happen.

When I wanted to leave my job, I was scared. I made good money, and at the time, I did not have another position lined up. I knew that if I left, there was a good chance we'd lose the house. My daughter was off at college at this point, but I still had my son living with me, and I wanted my daughter to have a place to come home to on breaks. I finally was no longer afraid when I realized we had a backup plan. I had a friend who owned a large farmhouse, and she said that if anything happened, we could live with them. I knew she meant it, so I was finally ready to leave.

While I was still at my old job, I entered a writing contest. You wrote about if you had a certain amount of money, what would you do with it? I wrote about how much I'd love to teach financial literacy and life skills to those in poverty. (Of course, I didn't use that terminology then because I didn't know it.) The prompt also asked to write about your experience with poverty. I wrote about my ex-husband and his drug addiction. I wrote about the time my van was repossessed because we couldn't afford payments. I wrote about all of these difficult things I'd been through, but how I'd use them to make the world a little better. I won! I used the money to buy a brand-new refrigerator.

That writing was so important to me because I actually got in trouble at work for writing about my past. I got in trouble for sharing my own story! I don't remember the exact reason why I got in trouble; maybe they never told me. But I just remember them saying it was inappropriate. As much as it sucked at the time, I now get to use that same story to help others.

I actually first got involved with Second Harvest through Forward STEPS. My former classmate from high school worked there, and she asked me to come in and help teach a class. We taught everyone about canning. We made and canned salsa that night, and it was so much fun.

When I came in for my interview for my current job at Second Harvest, I knew several of the people there. It felt like meeting with friends, and that's how I knew it was the perfect fit. When my now-boss called to tell me when I'd start (she didn't bother asking if I wanted the position), I was thrilled. I came in for my first day, and the then CEO and President came to see me, and he asked, "Where's your cape?" I asked what he meant, and he explained that from everything he'd heard, I must be Superwoman.

I love my job at Second Harvest because now I get to be *Superwoman* for others. I get to help them find and take advantage of all of these great resources that are out there to help people like us. I get to meet with people of the community who are going through exactly what I went through, and I get to help them. I get to pay it forward. I get to be their hope.

The Whitely Community: Strong in Culture and History

Ken Hudson's Story as Told to Amanda Hunter

G rowing up in a single parent household taught me a few things: first, you are not going to get everything you want; second, you will probably share a room until your roommate becomes of age and moves out; third, you're going to need to get a job to help out with expenses; fourth, be prepared for your brother's hand-me-downs; and fifth, there will be plenty of love and attention to go around.

Yes, I grew up in a poor family; although, I didn't discover this until I was in my twenties. My mother was handicapped and could not work, therefore she applied for government assistance, and we were raised on food stamps. Me, my brother, and two sisters were later joined in our small two-bedroom home, that had a make-shift room in the basement, by my mom's brother and his five kids. They would eventually rent a house across the street from us until my uncle's untimely death, which meant three of my cousins would come back to stay with us again.

We lived in a neighborhood that was heavily populated with a good mix of all types of people with different levels of economic status. There weren't any large, subsidized housing apartments in my neighborhood, but there was Section-8 housing and plenty of under-served families. The neighborhood had its share of small single-family owned corner stores that attempted to supply us with day-to-day and nutritional needs. Our family had its own challenges.

I think about the community I grew up in, and often find similarities between it and the Whitely neighborhood. For instance, Whitely people are generous and often give back in some way, whether it is with a neighborhood organization, their child's school, or at their church. They may not always be able to give their money, but they will give their time if you ask them to. The people here are very friendly and will invite you into their personal space quickly once they feel a common bond with you. With ten churches in the Whitely neighborhood alone, faith is an important element in most families, this I can personally relate with. In Whitely, everyone knows how to cook! Many of the residents enjoy fishing as a pastime activity. Many Whitely residents aspire to start their own businesses and many of them have tried and have been successful. This neighborhood has a rich history and many stories to tell.

Absent from the community is public and private resources that help to create a healthy community when present. Resources that feed the community and cause it to thrive and grow. Resources that help create healthy habits within the family structure and even serve to decrease stress. Although grocery stores were once within and near to the neighborhood, they are no longer within one mile of the neighborhood. This has negatively affected the availability of fresh fruits and vegetables for families young and old. There have been several attempts to remedy the absence of fresh produce by the neighborhood association and local groups, from mobile farm stands to popup gardens, and even neighborhood food pantries. None of these attempts will have the lasting effects of a local market that offers fresh produce daily.

The Whitely neighborhood has inadequate access to healthcare, which includes dental and pharmaceutical. The neighborhood is considered a medical desert! The lack of access to healthcare can contribute to far greater consequences within the community. With

African Americans being diagnosed at a higher rate for diseases such as stroke, various cancers, asthma, heart diseases, HIV/AIDS, and diabetes, the risks are greater when such resources are absent and otherwise not used. Patient-provider relationships suffer from perceived discrimination, medical mistrust, and poor communication and if residents never see a doctor, basic information and education is never transferred. Indoor gathering spaces are also needed for recreation activities. This would benefit young and old residents.

Many families have a need for some type of financial counseling or coaching. Programs of this type are currently not in the area but are needed along with other social help programs that would benefit individuals and families trying to change their current condition as it relates to economic health and wealth.

As you can see, food insecurity is not the only problem in the Whitely neighborhood, and for some it is not the most significant. Societal problems and their solutions are always deeper than we can see, and require us to look further and dig deeper than just under the surface. We must realize that when families struggle, the undeniable, inevitable result is that the neighborhood is going to struggle; and to build the community up, we must figure out what will help it grow. This is how we start to solve the problems we see and want to change.

The Whitely neighborhood has a rhythm that beats like an old southern church hymn or a negro spiritual. It is everlasting and resilient in all its ways, and will continue to beat for its children to sing for years into the future; the elders of the community will ensure it. Finding solutions to its woes will take time and courage, but with steadiness and thoughtful consideration the community will succeed and thrive, and the history and culture will be preserved for all to enjoy.

Did I Save the World Today?

Lisa Vernon's Story as told to Kellie Arrowood

I learned about the Poverty Simulation through Shafer Leadership Academy (*I'm a big fan!*). Open Door Health Services encourages its employees to go to their trainings. I usually feel empowered when learning new ideas to implement at work and in my personal life. I advocated for others to join me at this training, and so my co-worker Nancy decided to go with me.

We didn't know what to expect. Something like a game, but more to get an idea of what those we serve are going through. When we arrived at the Ross Community Center, we were directed into the gym area. There were tables all around the room, with irregular groupings of chairs in the middle. We walked in and received our tags and had to find our seats.

I was sitting with two other people (neither of them had been to a simulation before either). We started looking through the packet that included a description of our family unit, laying out the roles we would be playing and what "resources" we had. Brief descriptions of some limitations to navigate. I had a job! *Okay!* I looked around our "town" and at the "businesses" circling around the room: Grocery

Store, School, Employer, Homeless Shelter, etc. Our "neighborhood" was a cluster of chairs (houses) with other "families" in them.

Nancy, was all alone. Sitting in her chair in a "family" of one, reading her packet with no one else.

When our "week" started, I had to get to work but we were still trying to figure out our plan. By the time we figured out what we were doing, I was late to work and got laid off!

I thought, *I have to have a job! We won't make it!*

My partner was already staying at home with our two children to save money on transportation costs. I needed all of the transportation passes to get around to look for a job and even be at work. I knew it wasn't real, but I started getting caught up in it. I started feeling anxious. I didn't want to let my "family" down. I literally started sweating!

I did eventually get re-hired by the employer . . . but by then our transportation passes ran out. I was going nuts. This was crazy. How am I supposed to do anything without a job? I can't get to my job because I didn't have the right passes to travel there. I was so frustrated. My heart started pounding. I was going to fail this. It wasn't real, but I wanted to succeed. I could/can do this. I ran to an "agency" where I could get some help with those tickets to success. I tried to talk to the guy at the desk and he IGNORED ME! He was taking pictures! WHAT IS GOING ON?! I can survive this if I could just get some help and then I could get back to work. That employer wasn't going to take another excuse. I needed help!

I was trying to be nice to the agency person in the moment, because I didn't know what would happen if I wasn't. Would I fail because this person wouldn't even listen to me? All that anger and frustration was welling up inside.

Then it hit me. I understood what others must feel like when they just want to get past whatever obstacle is in front of them. On to the next thing. Struggling to just succeed in this one thing. This "make it or break it" moment. Okay, now I see why patients get loud . . . to be heard!

I saw Nancy and chatted with her real quick. She was scrambling, too. She was nervous that she was going to fail. It was like watching another person trying not to drown. The pace was hectic and we only got to exchange a brief couple of sentences. She was a seventy-eight-year-old man living alone and would have run out of money earlier, but she had overheard a single mom with three or four kids talking, and approached her—letting her know she would baby sit and got $10 to help stay in it to survive a little longer; keep going.

It's these relationships with other people, the mutual exchanges for survival, that allowed people in poverty to make it through.

It all boiled down to a complete lack of resources! Our patients struggle with a lack of resources. People struggle when they have this overwhelming pressure not to fail; not to be seen as a failure. They get short tempered, and little things, like making a phone call to say they were going to be late, seem like an impossible task when they don't have enough minutes or data left on their phone. They arrive fifteen minutes late after doing everything they can to even get there (those transportation tickets are hard to come by sometimes, aren't they?!) only to be told they have to reschedule by someone who drove to work and has perfectly manicured nails and cute shoes on today—while they themselves didn't have enough time or energy to do anything but arrive in what they wore to bed last night!

I feel all of this as that agency guy continues to ignore me. I had a few choice words for him. An angry outburst contained for the sake of a few dollars' worth of help!

I had experienced some of these feelings of helplessness myself when my husband passed. Isolation and struggle . . . mentally and financially. I was on food stamps. But when my car broke down (my transportation ticket), a family member loaned me theirs. I had people who would help me. No, I had people that could help me. As a matter of fact, the day of the Poverty Simulation I had just gotten a new car. Which is where I went after the simulation was over and just started sobbing.

When I think about where I am and what I do, I wonder "did I save the world today?" No. I didn't. There are so many hills I could die on, BUT I can help the person who I am talking to on the phone. One person at a time. Giving 100% of me, in the moment, to each one. I feel that each person deserves to be heard. Their story is everything in the moment, to them. I listen. I pick out the things that get jumbled up with emotion and usually after ten minutes of really hearing what they are saying, I find a place where I can help ease their stress just a little. Sometimes that is all it takes. People deserve to be heard.

I remember when Open Door told me about the position I have now, and how I'd be moving to the corporate offices downtown. I was a little overwhelmed by that thought.

I remember my early days of that drive. Seeing people on the downtown streets. Thinking how hard it must be walking in the rain to catch a bus with a soaked stroller filled with a fussy baby and groceries. Or the guy talking to no one else—was he high, mentally ill, or both? Then there was that older gentleman who was always so sad looking. His face. His body. The worn-out way he moved. Every part of him said sadness.

Every day I saw them, coming and going to work. Cry worthy moments happening just outside my car.

And then, one day I saw that gentleman smiling. It lit up my whole day! I knew I was right where I needed to be.

I get to help our patients transition from frustrated mad, to feeling heard and sort through the reasons "why." I get a chance to effect a change for the person I am listening to, and sometimes create change within our organization when there needs to be an exception to hard and fast rules.

Do I save the world? No. But I will take every opportunity—every chance—to learn more, do more, be more, and make here a better place to be.

HOPE IS A LUXURY

A POEM BY KELLIE ARROWOOD

Hope is a luxury, not given into easily—
Such a frightening thing Hope is.

Reaching out repeatedly only to have it
Dissipate again and again.
Flitting in nature
Between the heavenly grace of an angel
And a torturing specter of "I told you so"

It is a private thing for me
Not oft spoken.

Along comes a brilliant shining welcoming ray of possibility,
Calming reassurances of support
Offered in willingness
To instill a sense of belonging
To that *Dream of Hope*

Nurturing bonds from a new web of well-being
Replacing the old ties of reliance.

Free to dream of what's to become of me
And those I lead;
Taking hold of a child's hand
I step
Each day into leadership,
Showing him another world
Where moments are spent
In possibilities removed of old ways.
Dreams of what could be.

This poem originally appeared in *Facing Poverty* (2012), a publication
of The Facing Project that was organized by TEAMwork for Quality
Living in Muncie, Indiana.

THE MOST BEAUTIFUL PLACE

KELLIE ARROWOOD'S STORY AS TOLD TO JACKSON EFLIN

I wrote *Hope is a Luxury* more than a decade ago, for *Facing Poverty* back in 2012.

When it was being developed inside of me, I had just gotten out of Passage Way, a transitional housing program for domestic violence survivors. When I went into the emergency shelter my little family was split apart. One son was in the YOC, and one was couch surfing. Right about time for me to move out of the emergency shelter, I broke my leg and ended up in a wheelchair. The emergency shelter staff asked if I wanted to stay at their transitional housing apartments while I healed. I did. All my boys came to live with me there. We were together again.

When my third son entered kindergarten, the school nurses said that if I didn't get him on Adderall she would pursue neglect charges on me. Looking after all of them, all at once, took a lot of work.

While at Passage Way, I joined Circles and took the *Getting Ahead* classes. I worked hard to get ahead. I stayed for eighteen months. When I left Passage Way, I had "allies" who were shining rays of possibility. When I wrote the poem, I was still learning how to replace my old transactional ways of poverty for a sense of belonging to the community. When I couldn't pay my bills and was prepared to sell everything I had (I'd done it before), they all chimed that they had things they wouldn't mind getting rid of. We had a big rummage sale at an ally's house. My bills got paid. I was groovin' along.

Then I took my abuser back. He had changed! He even went to the Circles Cafe with me volunteering, helping. His addiction was better than me. Eventually, I felt strong enough to kick my ex out again. For the (almost) last time. That's when I wrote that poem.

I fled the area. Moved to southern Indiana and found the most beautiful place in the world. Got a solid job at the prison, even though I literally crawled up the steps of my house every night. I left my eleven-year-old son at home and prayed the prison wouldn't go on lock down. It was killing me. I *needed* help. I wanted so desperately to stay. My ex was doing better. Really this time he was. He was sober, he was in therapy and what not, so I thought, *He's done it!* I invited him to come down. And then he got a good job so I wouldn't have to crawl home every night. I was a stay-at-home mother and no more Adderall! One of the first SMART Goals my youngest son ever set, worked toward and achieved!

His father's help/income meant I had time/energy for a vegetable garden so big—it took hours to water it. It was massive. I would get up every morning and make coffee and his breakfast. Pack his lunch. I would hang the laundry outside in the sunshine (to save money on the electric bill). I would watch the deer eat my broccoli. I would hunt mushrooms with the neighbor. There was a bull that would come in our yard from time to time. A big ol' ring in its nose, and there was a man with his stubby cigar who had to herd the bull back where it was supposed to be. Crackin' his whip, *whap-ish!* And my son would go out to wait for the school bus, the owls still hooting before dawn. And oh, I loved that place.

But eventually—just past my notice, he isolated me. And then he isolated me even more. Soon my car wasn't my car anymore. My phone didn't get paid. I'd piggyback Wi-Fi from my neighbor. And then, that dreaded day.

Nine months later, when my youngest son Kodi and I were hiding in his room with the door locked, that man ripped it off its hinges. Like a "here's Johnny" moment. A few friends helped me sneak everything out a window. I made like I was doing the grocery run so he would give me at least $100, what we lived off of for a household of three (including his weekly alcohol and other medications). I snuck away, and came back to Muncie. Humiliated and ashamed of me.

This time I was able to pick up the pieces *quickly*.

Everyone I knew from Circles—Dorica, Molly, and Karen—knew how much I loved it there, and they all surrounded me with love and acceptance. "You know the steps," they told me. "So, let's get busy." And I did. I joined AmeriCorps as a VISTA, and from there I got a job at Second Harvest, the organization that had taken over doing the Circles and *Getting Ahead Program*. And everything was going great. I was filled with hope and felt like I was finally coming into my own.

And then there was a new setback.

I'd been preparing for all my sons to be out of my house. The last of them, my youngest, was growing up. Nineteen years old and he was going to be moving out soon. He had a job. A savings. A girl. I was preparing for what the world would be like after he moved out. I hadn't prepared for him to die.

I didn't know how to go on. My "team" of support knew. They knew the life had been sucked out of me. They knew my purpose had been this and then it was gone. He's gone. This group of friends and allies I had developed from Circles and *Getting Ahead*, they arranged the funeral, took me to a counselor. They mourned with me. They missed him, too. I didn't bounce back. I didn't want to do this! How does one DO THIS? I tried to go back to work. Ended up getting blood clots from curling up in my bed and little else. And still my team supported me. Many of my coworkers gave me their vacation hours, gave me grace to get myself back to better.

The difference between the me that entered that shelter and the me who sits here today is that I do have that community of support. People who didn't just give me a few dollars to make it through today, but allies that poured love into me *and* my sons. They became a part of our family. Loved me unconditionally. That is the difference. This connection to my community is lasting.

It's taken a bit to get my hope back.

The last ten years have changed me, and my relationship with hope. It is hope that has brought me back from despair. Hope, that has time and time again sustained me through my darkest moments.

I hope to inspire others. To show up and provide help to those who need it today, and give a sense of hope for tomorrow.

HOPE IS A LUXURY I GROW FOR MYSELF

A POEM BY KELLIE ARROWOOD

When I think about hope now, I think about
The way it fills the space
Once taken up by *anxiety* and *fear*.

I think further ahead

And make plans for future versions
Of *myself*.

Hope grows within me
Each day.

Before my feet hit the floor,
I move into a mindset:

"Make it happen.

No matter what."

Some days, I wake weeping,

"Loss, *oh loss*,
You wretched thing!"

this *grief*–
A *thief* to my soul!

***

I am armed with the knowledge that,
on this day, if I *run* too low,

I can *turn to my team*: my gang gets me.

In my *mind*, I *imagine*

Hope is a *seed*.
I *plant* inside of me.
Only my own *hands*
Can place it there.

My own *determination*
Coaxes *life*

From that tiny, precious thing.

Oh—But every eye can see

These *hopes*, these *dreams*:

Blossoming reality.

WHAT KEEPS US ALIVE

AN ANONYMOUS STORY AS TOLD TO JACQUELINE HANOMAN

When thinking about resource insecurity, I used to think about Maslow's hierarchy—food, shelter, clothing, water, all of that. Obviously, these are important, and now I realize that through relationships, love, connection—that out of these secure attachments with others—these needs will be met. I think about the little children I have seen who are fed, who are clothed, but who weren't hugged, who weren't touched, and I see the blankness in their eyes. They would die because they lacked these essential physical needs.

I grew up seeing more emotional resource insecurity than basic needs insecurity. Life turned upside down when I finished high school. My parents got divorced and they left the church where they pastored. They were both pastors and their divorce led to emotional distress within the congregation.

There is a quote from Anne Lamott which I can't remember exactly, but it's something along the lines of: "If you haven't known that there is some darkness in this world, or there is difficulty, pain, suffering by the time you are 18, you aren't human." And I always think that I witnessed pain for others, but the pain for me happened when I turned 18.

My parents were best at loving us, but not in their marriage. They worked beautifully together, but my parents didn't hug, nor were they affectionate as a couple. Today my parents have a lot of respect for and are kind to each other, but they are not friends from my perspective. My dad has a mental illness, and when I was a teen he kept going off the rails, and my mom gave him an ultimatum to work on their marriage. The ultimatum was asking my dad to either go to therapy together, to work on their marriage, and if he didn't put the work in, she would leave him. Instead of working on the marriage, my dad pulled further away from my mom, and really from our whole family.

I had amazing friends, and they were the ones who showed up when my parents got divorced, not the adults. My friend group showed up for me when I was 18, when my parents separated. My parents told me I couldn't tell anybody, because of being pastors. They were going to therapy to work on their marriage and the therapist told them that I needed to tell someone, so I told my best friend. She was there for me when my dad was bizarre and acting off. She saw all of this and told me, "I'm so sorry, this is Crazy town, but it will be ok. We will be ok."

That's probably why I see resource insecurity as ultimately when you don't have people, because for me, the pain and the trauma around that was the people that were silent and never talked to me; people who had loved me my whole life. I mean my youth pastor, my children's pastor, none of them came to me and said anything. We had a youth group of about three-hundred. I led worship every Sunday. Nobody came to me and asked me how I was doing, except for my friends.

So, I think about resources as people. Sometimes just a smile, a kind greeting. That is so important for me; how we greet people. When you walk into a space and you see how the space is, how people greet you.

I like to be present when things happen. Just to show up for people and not be freaked out by emotions. My parents, even in their brokenness, just showed up for people. It was always modeled for me. Even in our dysfunction, we showed up for people.

When I could have been hungry, when I could have been unhoused, I had family who supported us. I am aware of my privilege. I try to live my life as someone who listens to the people in my life. When I think about resource insecurity, I think sometimes it's the person not having another person. Each person can identify what that is for them, but I think anytime someone is resource insecure, for me its basic form is when they don't have *the thing* they need to be at least somewhat stable, whether it is feeling stable, or having what they need to do the next thing in their life. That's kind of what I see it as. Insecurity. Being able to make choices, being able to focus. I think our brains, our bodies can't work as effectively as they could if they don't have the people, the food, the housing, the clothing that they feel they need to be themselves.

Thinking again about the children who would die from not having those emotional attachments I think whatever that power is, I think it is a physiological need that we all have. There is something that happens to us when we look at each other in the eye but being culturally sensitive, that may not be the thing. When we see each other, whatever that looks like, and we are present for each other, whether that's through touch, whether that's through a listening ear, whether that's through saying "What do you need?" and the person saying "I need you to be here."

I do think that being accurate when empathizing with someone so they feel most at ease, especially when facing something challenging, is powerful. Even in the good, if there is no one to celebrate you getting a job, or you having a child, or getting a degree, to be there for you when you move to a new place, that also can cause, what is that called, *detachment*, it can also cause trauma, if somebody is not there in the good things, now that I think more about it. That example of the babies, that is an extreme example, but yeah, we know babies need that physical touch, we know that skin to skin, how powerful that can be. And I know, I experienced that firsthand. I didn't do that with my first child. It wasn't even brought up at that time by doctors, lactation consultants, or nurses. But I did it with my second, and it was pretty amazing. Each child is different, each person is different, so my first child might have resisted it, I don't know. But with my second, we were securely attached, nobody could come between us, because she needed me for that time in her life.

Even in extreme cases, I think emotional attachments keep people alive longer. I think of the earthquake that happened recently in Turkey and Syria. It was a terrible earthquake where buildings collapsed and I heard an interview with a woman, and it was conducted when she was in her rawest state, and there was still no relief. Yet she had hope that help was coming, that other nations would come to help, that the U.S. would help, that nations nearby would help. And you could hear the terrible trauma in her voice, that they had to leave people, leave their loved ones in this collapsed building to get to safety. And yet I know from the way she was talking that she was with some people too, and they could make the choice together. That was just the worst choice you could make and she was crying, and at the end she still had something to say. She thanked those who were helping and she pleaded for people to come to their aid. And because some of the things I know of how trauma works, is that if someone can still ask something of somebody, all the negative stuff of trauma hasn't set in yet. There is still the belief that somebody will show up. I think that thinking and believing that somebody will show up, believing "we can get through this," keeps people alive longer.

People keep us alive. Relationships keep us alive. Secure attachments. We need each other to stay alive.

FIGHTING TO PROVE WHO I AM

AN ANONYMOUS STORY AS TOLD TO CARRIE BRADSHAW

I 've been my true self for about a decade now, which has been a beautiful experience, but it has certainly come with its challenges. I've experienced love, but also hate. Both of these have come from outside my community and from within. Sometimes, the world just doesn't know what to do with a trans woman.

I was born and raised in southern California. For the longest time, I thought I was just your standard gay kid. At fifteen, my guidance counselor started to introduce me to the idea of being transgender. I spent about six months presenting myself as feminine before I came out to my mother. From then on, while she was very supportive, she was also overbearing. She was afraid of the outside world and what it would do to a young trans person.

My first high school asked me to leave. They said I was a distraction to the other students. This was the first time I had had to think about what my being transgender meant to those around me.

Over the next year, year and a half, I saw eight therapists. In order to begin treatments, I had to prove to the insurance company that I was in fact trans. I finally found Dr. O at a children's hospital in Los Angeles. My insurance required a letter from her and my therapist, but it was finally enough.

I've since moved to Indiana, and the insurance scenario has only gotten harder. I am currently on my mother's insurance, but because they are in California, any treatments I go through have to be in California. I recently got back from a medical trip to L.A. I found a lump in my breast, and I was concerned that it may be breast cancer. (The irony of developing breast cancer from trying to grow breasts!) I stopped taking my progesterone out of fear, but, of course, abruptly stopping a medication I had been on for so long caused debilitating side effects. I was depressed, anxious. I was going two or three days without eating. I was getting at most four hours of sleep. Luckily, the lump was a cyst, so Dr. O okayed me to continue my medication, just on a different schedule.

This recent scare has brought to light another fear that is looming on the horizon. In September, I will be twenty-six, which means I will no longer be on my mother's insurance. So far, I've had no luck in finding a new provider. Many providers have reached out to me, but as soon as they hear that I am trans, they say that they don't know how to help me. Without insurance, I will not be able to afford my medication, the medication that my body has been on for so long, that it doesn't know how to function without it. The thought has crossed my mind to start rationing my pills for when the day comes. This comes with its own dangers.

I know that many people, inside and outside of the community, think that it is so easy for trans people these days. That we can just call a doctor and get any medication we want sent right over for free. That's just not the reality. There is so much red tape and waiting lists and paperwork just to be my authentic self.

Insurance and medication are not the only resources my community is lacking. Since moving from California to Indiana, I have experienced the lack of another vital resource—knowledge.

I am open about my identity, but that brings a lot of controversy. People ask so many ignorant questions. Countless times, I have been at work, in a professional setting, and someone will blatantly ask me about what is between my legs. Something so personal, in front of our coworkers. You would never ask a cisgendered person about their genitals, but because I'm trans, they think it's okay. They don't understand that when they do this, they have ripped me out of that professional standing.

While California still struggles, it is drastically ahead of Indiana. The acceptance of transgender people is still so new in Indiana. The structure was so different in California— the efficiency, the knowledge, the organizations. I was a part of several organizations back in California to help educate the public, but that's just not a thing here yet.

I've thought about being a more public figure, a voice for the trans community. I want to help people understand what it means to be trans and the experiences we go through. I want to help answer the questions I have received out of pure ignorance, and not in an intentionally harmful way, but just in a lack of knowledge kind of way. I want those people to have a safe space to ask those questions and to learn and grow. It's so important to have a place to have that dialogue, but that's not happening here in Indiana—it's just people fighting against people.

There are parts of my story that would make for an excellent spokesperson. I've been openly trans for ten years now. I've experienced the hate and the love. I am able to let people say hateful things to me and let it not bother me. But I also worry that I'm not the right spokesperson. Within my community, I am considered privileged. I am "passing," which means that unless I told you, you would never know that I am trans. I *look* like a woman. Because of this, some people within the trans community believe that I am not able to truly understand the hatred that we often go through.

I have spent the past decade fighting to prove who I am. I've had to have countless doctors sign off to the insurance companies to say that I'm trans. I've had to prove to my classmates that I'm a woman without being distractingly so. I've had to travel back and forth across the country to receive medical care. I've had to prove to my own community that I belong. While I do not feel the need to get the world's approval, the world still requires it.

HONORING THE BIRTHDAY CAKE

MELINDA'S STORY AS TOLD TO PETER KAMAJIAN

How wonderful it is to help! I smile internally as the cashier scans my items at the grocery—can after can of green beans, fruit cocktail, and condensed soup, all at retail price. *Doesn't it feel great to be helping*, I repeat to myself as I heft the bags and make my way to the car. *It's time to make a difference*, I promise as I walk under the office banner that announces this week's food drive. I deposit my payload of cans onto the ever-growing pile of similar foods, all canned or boxed, shelf-stable and highly processed. My good deed completed, satisfied that I was able to improve the lives of (hopefully) a dozen or so people with my contribution, I move on to my work for the day.

As a sociologist, caring about the problems of the world is the focal point of my career. Acting on such problems is a natural impulse; of course, I already do that every time a food drive rolls around. As I study societal issues on a grand scale, however, I can't help but feel like I could be doing *more*. It's common knowledge in my field that food insecurity is a symptom of larger institutional problems, and given the massive scale of hunger in America, it gnaws at me that there might be a more efficient way of helping stop it—should I be buying way more cans? Handing food out myself? Neither of these seem sustainable given my time, budget, and the scale of the problem.

One evening I did a little research, and discovered a local food bank that hosts a program which seems promising—it says its goal is to stop hunger not just by giving out food but by teaching people how to break out of the cycle of hunger and poverty. The idea of "Help for Today AND Hope for Tomorrow" really resonated with me. I'd spent so much effort giving people fish and feeding them for a day—was this the proper way to teach them to fish and feed them for a lifetime?

I'm excited to see inside a food bank—having given so many cans over the years, I look forward to seeing where they all end up before distribution. I'm expecting a pile of packaged products in a storage room somewhere, possibly adjoined to the food bank's offices. When I arrived, however, that perception vanished; numerous semi-trucks rolled past my windshield as I pulled in, connecting to the same building I was told contained the food bank offices. I get inside, and after some introductions I am taken into the warehouse. What I encounter makes my jaw drop; my preconceived notion of the scale of food bank operations are completely shattered.

A sea of ceiling-high shelves stretches out before me, each stacked with multitudes of food and supplies. I see an empty space on one shelf, easily large enough to contain twice my yearly contribution of cans. I feel like a speck of dust in such a huge space, and the realization of how small my donations have been in the grand scheme of things is instantly humbling. Notably, very little of the food stored here is canned; if it is, those cans are stacked together and wrapped on massive pallets. Taking in the panoply of food before me, I know there is indeed much more I should be doing.

A few weeks have passed since that initial induction. I've spent that time working with volunteers at the food bank, organizing food to be distributed and learning the intricacies of the fight against hunger. I learned that, while still helpful, my full-retail method of donating cans is far from efficient—giving the cash I *would've* spent on cans would allow the food bank to obtain significantly more material from farm and wholesale sources. It's also here that I encounter some differences in the way people perceive food donation.

We stand around a table loaded with food. Myself and the other dozen or so volunteers are chatting about the various options available to recipients, and I recognized an unsettling amount of judgment coming from others and, indeed, myself.

The spread of food includes lots of sugary bakery items, like donuts and birthday cakes. Coincidentally, these items are the most demanded from the people we're giving them to—as I listen to the continued requests for these baked goods, I can't help but think *wouldn't it be better if you went after the healthier stuff?* And I'm not alone—I overheard several people wondering the same thing. In a life where nutrition can be scarce, why opt for the item that's full of carbs and sugar?

I knew this way of thinking was wrong, but I couldn't quite articulate why—and then it hit me. When grocery money is tight, birthday cakes are a luxury; however, every kid is taught that you celebrate a birthday with cake. The two are so intrinsically linked in our culture that having a cake-less birthday—or even a birthday with no sweets whatsoever—is indicative of something being wrong with your celebration. Does falling below a certain level of income mean you stop having birthdays? The people here to receive food are aware that cake isn't very nutritious; it's the *cultural value* of having access to these kinds of goods that makes a difference. Sometimes the help is also the hope and it comes in the form of a birthday treat.

Returning from my time at the food bank, I feel humbled—not just by the scale of their operations, but by the realization of my own misconceptions and judgments. Who am I to put my own nutritional outlook on strangers receiving food? Sentimentality is a personal thing, and I have to accept that different foodways are meaningful to different people. Armed with this new perspective, I grapple with discovering my true role in the world of food distribution. As an educator and researcher, one thing is for certain: I need to think a lot bigger than "cans."

As time passes, I incorporate more work on food insecurity in my classes and discussions with other academics. At conferences, I do my best to enlighten my peers about how they can help, especially those who may have not had the experience of large-scale food distribution. My role as an educational leader is to bring these issues into the public consciousness. Every choice we make impacts the supply chain. Everything matters from the systemic nature of food insecurity to the simple fact that every kid deserves the affirmation, celebration, and hope of a birthday cake.

EAT THE COOKIE

AN ANONYMOUS STORY AS TOLD TO KRISTA WISE

D amn it. The Starbucks drive thru again?! Are you kidding me? Ughhh. Resist. The. Cookie. And then I ask myself, *why?* I affirm, I deserve the cookie.

Lack mentality isn't something new for me. Generations before me suffered from this beast of burden that bound us to poverty. Never knowing if there would be another cookie, or the funds to buy one. Perhaps it was all monetary restrictions that plagued our dreams, unaware of the real lack of resource, emotional security. A resource insecurity that ran like a river through our family history.

I grew up in a quaint little town in Indiana, where most families knew their neighbors. Me though, I never had the opportunity to meet one of the most important people in my life. My father was in the military which sent him miles from my mother and me when I was a baby. I was too young to form an opinion about the situation which left many unanswered questions as to why he never returned. I asked my mother when "curiosity got the cat," but I still felt unfulfilled knowing there's always two sides to every story. I can now reflect on how hard this must have been for my mother to have a newborn crying for love and support as she cried herself for her own lack of emotional security with my father being gone.

Eventually my mother moved on, to someone barely older than me. This closeness in age presented many obstacles that led to me feeling unheard and unprotected. This emotional baggage started collecting on the inside and visibly showing on the outside. My weight climbed higher the more I felt the need to protect myself and conceal my emotions. I found solace in food.

My mother noted this weight gain, I know by her continuous comments about how big I was getting. Never taking the time to reflect on why. Maybe she didn't have the emotional awareness inside herself to even see she should be asking deeper questions instead of making hurtful comments. These comments only fed my lack of self-esteem, and made me feel on my own.

I barely made it out of high school, left home as soon as possible, and inevitably had my first child at nineteen. A pattern. I found myself alone, the child's father inactive. Another pattern. Then I met my soulmate. A man that loves me and stands up for me. A man that helped me see my worth. Now when I stand up to him and he gets frustrated I say, "Hey you asked for this!" which sends us both into laughter and makes me feel like the luckiest girl in the world.

It hasn't been easy for us. As an interracial couple we used to feel the scrutiny from others, my family included, which drove a wedge between us and the family, but it only magnetized us closer together.

My love and I, we had fun. Maybe a little too much fun as we both found ourselves in active addiction. The partying was fun while it lasted, but the emotional wounds we were hiding were still there. My family was sure I was an angel and he had brainwashed me, leading to distance and conflict with my family when I needed them most. I had to learn to love them from afar, and my husband and I were pulled closer together.

One day I decided, "that's it, no more, I'm done living this way." I was ready to make a change from an addict's lifestyle no matter what my husband decided. To my delight, he followed suit the next day, and we never looked back.

That's nine years ago now. It seems like a lifetime ago, because it was. I have a whole new life now. I'm thankful for those kind souls who did reach out to me during this time to help me transition. I believe the universe sends the people you need in your life in divine timing. My degree from Ball State University is a powerful reminder of that.

When I got clean and sober and finally started losing the weight, I felt confident enough to search for my father. I craved to know the answers to my questions and build a relationship with the man I never got to meet. I did reach out, and received a message in return from his new wife. "I'm sorry, he died last week." This was obviously not the response I had hoped for, but sometimes the universe gives you what you need, not what you want. This effort to connect was not without fruit though, as his wife explained he had a brother that had always wanted to connect with me, but didn't out of respect for his brother. Now I do have the chance to feel somewhat connected to my father through his brother which has been healing for me.

So here I am, a new me. No longer lacking emotional insecurity from others because I found it in myself. I am one-hundred pounds lighter, literally, of physical and emotional baggage. I have found the confidence in myself to know I no longer need food to fill an emotional void or to protect myself. I now have the confidence that I will have the resources that I need, and that I know how to refrain from overindulgence to fill emotional gaps.

My husband and I are active in our community working to help others overcome substance abuse and resource deficits. We feel fulfilled. And now I no longer fight with myself when he pulls up in that drive-thru lane. I eat the cookie.

The Overflow

Marilynn Collier's Story as Told to Lisa Vernon

S omeone asked me recently about when the Lord called me to ministry. I traveled through my mind trying to recall the answer to the question and for the life of me I could not find it. I don't ever remember a time in my life where I didn't feel called to serve God, or was not able to hear that still small voice in my soul that I recognized as my Heavenly Father's. As a matter of fact, my lifelong friend, Frank, would swear that I was ordained as a child! He would admit that he and the other neighborhood kids were full of mischief and would even fight each other sometimes. He would go on to tell you that I would immediately stand up, call them to attention, and tell them to sit down and act like they had some sense because the Lord would not be pleased with them.

It wasn't until much later in life that I was "officially" ordained in the AME Zion church. I worked as a chaplain at St. Vincent in Anderson, Indiana, and then also started doing chaplain work at IU Ball in Muncie. Chaplain work is not for the faint of heart, but it is what God wanted me to be doing at that time. He used me to pray with, comfort, and minister to families and patients who were experiencing sickness, fear, turmoil, and sometimes death. It was emotionally draining and almost too much at times. I desperately wanted to be able to make everything better for these people and couldn't. It was so hard, but God was preparing me for an adventure.

My sixtieth birthday rolled around, and I knew what I wanted. I wanted a "gathering" of women. A time where strong, independent and intelligent women come together and celebrate each other for the "QUEENS" that we are. I expected fifty women to turn out. I was wrong. One hundred-and-fifty women showed up! The Gathering of the Queens was born.

We continued to meet and have never stopped. We took trips together, one to the Underground Railroad, we had meals together, we prayed together, we developed unbreakable bonds, and we formed a sisterhood in Christ. What a royal sisterhood! Of course, we encountered many challenges. The pandemic was our first one. It definitely put a wrench in things; but as resourceful, determined, united women, we found a way. We met at parks; stayed separated but still enjoyed each other's company. I was so grateful that God had placed these women into my life and me into theirs. I was so grateful that I knew we had to give back.

The community we live in, grew up in, and love is in a bad way. Drugs, alcohol, addiction, violence, shootings, homelessness, poverty, and hunger have reared their ugly heads, and God wanted us to do something. He gave us a vision and a hunger to make a difference.

The Queens began buying food to give to folks in need. I remember going shopping and having to limit what we bought because we were spending our own money. We needed hundreds of boxes of cereal but could only buy twelve. We took what we bought and set up shop in the elements. I can't say the weather was bad every time we had a giveaway, but I can say that Indiana gets stifling hot in the summer and freezing cold in the winters. There was a lot of shivering and a lot of sweating those three years we were outside, but we stood on God's Word and were amazed by all that we saw Him do. The limited supplies we used to buy have turned into entire skids that we get for free. Those twelve boxes of cereal have turned into hundreds of boxes of cereal.

In December of 2022, we gained walls! The Impact Center gave us space to operate a pantry. We went from having to rent two to three U-Hauls a week to getting a truck purchased for us by Mayor Broderick, and we have opened a second pantry in Anderson. We serve an average of eight-hundred families a month. The Queens serve much more than food. We serve love without judgment, acceptance without question, and allow God's light to shine through us. God has blessed our faithfulness. Luke 6:38 says, "Give and it shall be given to you; good measure, pressed down, shaken together, and running over." We are living in God's overflow, and I believe in my spirit He is far from done with what He's got planned for The Queen's Gathering and the city of Anderson.

My vision is for us to continue farming a piece of land that my mama gardened for over forty years and use it as a community garden. Teach folks to grow their own fruits and vegetables and to preserve them for the winter. Help them to be able to help themselves. Teach them so that they can teach their children. Go back to the basics! I thank God every single day for a mama that taught me to use the land to feed myself and how to not waste. Don't get me wrong, I celebrate progress. I love my cell phone and the wonders of technology BUT . . . maybe, just maybe, we could benefit from going back to the good ol' days and their good ol' ways. Put our focus on people, build people up, support one another, neighbor collaborate with neighbor, more selfless and less selfish.

My sisters and I will continue following God's Lead. We will love on each other and everybody we meet, we will stock shelves in the pantries, drive the truck to pick up thirty skids of free food, get dirty out in the garden, spread God's Light all over the streets of Anderson and thank God without ceasing for the overflow.

Resource Guide

Need Help Finding Resources?
Contact Forward STEPS, an initiative of Second Harvest Food Bank, at 765-287-8698 for help finding local resources.

<u>Local Food Pantries</u>
Find food pantries in Blackford, Delaware, Grant, Henry, Jay, Madison, Randolph, and Wabash Counties.

https://curehunger.org/get-help/

<u>Affordable Connectivity</u>
The Affordable Connectivity Program is a federal program that helps low-income households pay for internet service and connected devices like a laptop or tablet.

https://www.affordableconnectivity.gov/

<u>The Excel Center</u>
The Excel Center is a free public school for adults that gives adults the opportunity to earn an Indiana Core 40 high school diploma.

https://excelcenter.org/

Firefly Children and Family Alliance

Firefly empowers Hoosiers through a wide range of support programs and resources designed to give parents, children, and individuals everything they need to live successfully.

https://fireflyin.org/

Getting Ahead

Break the cycle of poverty with this free 16-week program involving rigorous work done in a safe learning environment with the support of an experienced facilitator.

https://curehunger.org/get-help/ready-to-get-ahead/

GLAAD

Find resources for LGBTQIA+ individuals and their families.

https://glaad.org/resourcelist/

Head Start

Head Start is a federal program that aims to enhance the cognitive, emotional, and social development of children from birth to age five from low-income families making sure they are school ready.

https://eclkc.ohs.acf.hhs.gov/

Indiana 211

2-1-1 is the State of Indiana Family and Social Services Administration's free and confidential service that helps Hoosiers across find the local resources. Call 2-1-1 for assistance.

Indiana Foreclosure Help and Mortgage Assistance

Several organizations and programs can help pay your mortgage while providing resources such as mediation, moratoriums, and free counseling. Additionally, there are non-profits that are HUD approved. Hoosiers facing foreclosure, whether immediate or in the distant future, may call 877-GET-HOPE for assistance.

Indiana Department of Workforce Development
The Indiana Department of Workforce Development connects people and employers.

https://www.in.gov/dwd/

PAF (Patient Advocate Foundation)
PAF Case Managers offer free, one-on-one support to patients and families to help them solve real-life problems related to a serious health condition. We help patients understand their choices to make healthy decisions for a strong recovery.

https://www.patientadvocate.org/connect-with-services/case-management-services-and-medcarelines/

SNAP
The Supplemental Nutrition Assistance Program (SNAP) provides food assistance to low- and no-income people and families living in the United States.

https://www.fns.usda.gov/snap/supplemental-nutrition-assistance-program

TANF
The Temporary Assistance for Needy Families (TANF) program provides help to low-income families with children to achieve economic self-sufficiency.

https://www.acf.hhs.gov/ofa/programs/temporary-assistance-needy-families-tanf

DISCUSSING THIS TOPIC IN YOUR COMMUNITY

BECAUSE The Facing Project is steeped in empathy and connecting across differences, *Listening Circles* are a fantastic way to bring more people into the conversation on the topics/themes addressed in this book.

Listening Circles provide readers with a more intimate experience to reflect upon the stories and ask questions in a controlled environment. However, it's important to include a trained facilitator who understands how to moderate, when to let conversations flow, and when to step in to move them along.

If you choose to include *Listening Circles* in your community, we recommend having at least four different locations and dates for these to happen, and be sure to have folks register in advance. Hosts could include area libraries, schools, and/or colleges and universities.

Also, it's important to set the following standards at the beginning of each discussion:

1. We acknowledge that we are all here to learn with open hearts and open minds.

2. Before speaking or asking a question, we all agree that we will take a moment to reflect on if "my voice/question matters in the particular moment" or if "I should give the opportunity to someone else to speak."

3. R-E-S-P-E-C-T is more than an Aretha Franklin song; respect is a value that we will hold close throughout our discussions.

4. We honor the storytellers who shared their experiences, and our goal is to not discount them but rather to understand how all of our stories are intertwined and part of the human condition.

Ideally, *Listening Circles* should have no more than 20 participants in each circle. If you find that one of your locations may have more than 20, you'll want to explore breaking them up into more than one group.

Also, participants should have read a copy of this book before participating. This makes for deeper discussion, and it keeps the facilitators from having to give a full breakdown of all of the themes/topics included throughout the book. More copies can be ordered at www.facingproject.com.

However, it's always good to open a *Listening Circle* with a reading of one or two stories that immediately follow introductions and community standards. Ask for one to two attendees to volunteer to read the selected stories aloud to the *Circle*.

Then have the facilitator ask the group: How did those two stories make you feel?

And be sure to have them follow-up with "tell me more" and other open-ended questions. Of course, a trained facilitator will understand how to let this process flow.

Lastly, be sure to include action items for the participants. This could include other events in your community centered around the topic/issues addressed in this book, volunteer opportunities with nonprofits, and/or other ways they can get involved.

About The Facing Project

The Facing Project is a 501(c)(3) nonprofit that creates a more understanding and empathetic world through stories that inspire action. The organization provides tools and a platform for everyday individuals to share their stories, connect across differences, and begin conversations using their own narratives as a guide. The Facing Project has engaged more than 7,500 volunteer storytellers, writers, and actors who have told more than 1,500 stories that have been used in grassroots movements, in schools, and in government to inform and inspire action. In addition, stories from The Facing Project are published in books through The Facing Project Press and are regularly performed on *The Facing Project Radio Show* on NPR.

- Learn more at facingproject.com.

- Follow us on Twitter and Instagram @FacingProject, and on Facebook at *TheFacingProject*.

THANKS TO OUR SPONSORS

www.ingramcontent.com/pod-product-compliance
Lightning Source LLC
Chambersburg PA
CBHW021129130726
47988CB00003B/1227